1&2 Peter

Grow in Grace

Sarah K. Howley

Flaming Dove Press

1&2 Peter: Grow in Grace

Flaming Dove Press
an imprint of
InspiritEncourage LLC
1520 Belle View Blvd #5081
Alexandria, VA 22307
www.inspiritencourage.com

ISBN 978-1-960793-33-1 (e-pub)
ISBN 978-1-960793-34-8 (paperback)
ISBN 978-1-960793-35-5 (large print)

Printed in the United States of America

Contents

Welcome

to this Study of 1&2 Peter

First and Second Peter were named after the most likely author of the book, the disciple Peter. The letters state that he wrote then in "Babylon", most likely a reference to Rome. Peter was first known as Simon, and the name change is recounted in three of the Gospels when Jesus called him Peter. This occurred when Simon, in faith, identified Jesus as the Messiah and His response was to rename Simon to Peter, meaning Rock. The Rock we build our lives upon had been named and we too stand on the Rock, Jesus, just as Simon did that day and ever more.

Peter wrote these letters to the churches throughout Asia Minor, which is modern-day Turkey. The Christians there were experiencing heavy persecution, and he wrote to encourage them in challenges, help them to grow in faith, live firmly in their identity, and look forward to the return of Christ. Peter wrote of hope in suffering and living in genuine faith and holiness as God's chosen people. Peter called the believers to be wary of false teachers and teachings and stand certain of the return of Christ. Peter repeatedly urged the believers to share Jesus' love and generosity despite the suffering they were undergoing.

The books refer to the Old Testament numerous times and offer insight into the riches of belonging in Christ that can be difficult to grasp. Leaning into these passages, Peter echoes how the Israelites were His people, though they were dispersed, just like those persecuted in Asia Minor were also spread throughout the area. These truths of the people of God in Exodus and other Old Testament verses are also there for us to claim in our own trials and troubles.

The sessions in this Bible study each open with warm-up questions, go on to a reading from 1 or 2 Peter and questions related to the passage. Then the study goes to the linked Old Testament passages and questions. Each study session ends with considerations for personal application. Additional tips and suggestions on approaching the study for individuals and groups follow.

Suggestions for this Study

This study is composed of 8 sessions and is designed for individual or small group study. It is written to spark thought and discussion of the Scripture, inviting individuals and groups seeking God to engage in meaningful conversations about the biblical text. For 'You will seek me and find me when you seek me with all your heart,' as Jeremiah 29:13 says.

General Guidelines for Individual Study

1. Open each session with prayer. Ask God to speak through his Word.

2. Respond to the Introduction questions to focus on the theme of the session and what Jesus says in the main reading.

3. Read the passage more than once. Using different translations can offer expanded viewpoints on the meaning of the original text. This study uses the New International Version (NIV) as the basis of questions and quotes. However, any version may be used to provide insight and assist in revealing meaning.

4. This study is designed to offer a starting point for the discovery of what God has to say to you through his Word. Because the study looks at how the Old Testament is reflected in the epistles, there are observation and interpretation questions about the readings in 1 and 2 Peter and then about the links in the Old Testament, as well as comparisons between the passages. These are followed by application questions for personal and group discussion. Writing your responses will provide clarity and focus your thoughts on the verses.

5. Use a Bible dictionary or other reference books to look up any unfamiliar words, places, or names.

General Guidelines for Group Study

1. Come to each session prepared. Some groups will choose to read and respond ahead of time then gather and discuss together; others will gather to read and discuss together. Before beginning, agree how the group would like to proceed so everyone can be prepared.

2. Be an active participant in the group by sharing your thoughts and responses to the questions. Groups often have members who are of varied maturity in Christ and each perspective should be valued.

3. Listen to each other. Consider the amount of time that is available for all to share and be careful not to dominate the conversation.

4. Be open. As there are various 'right' answers, be open to considering alternate viewpoints and agree to disagree.

5. Maintain confidentiality of the group. For participants to be willing to share and grow, the trust level in the group must be high. Do not share outside the group unless permission is given to do so.

6. Expect God to meet you in the study. His Word is living and active (Heb. 4:12) and he is present when we gather in his name (Matt. 18:20).

Introduction

The recipients of these letters were experiencing persecution and needed encouragement. What kind of persecution, or maltreatment and oppression, do Christians undergo today? What encouragement would you offer them? Consider those in your country as well as those who may live in environments hostile to Christianity.

Peter spoke extensively against false teachings, particularly those from Christian texts that may be misinterpreted. How would you explain to someone studying the Bible the best way to check their understanding of ideas presented in Scripture?

Session 1: Our Living Hope
1 Peter 1:1-12

Opening

How would you describe the difference between Christian hope and worldly wishes?

What practices or habits help you handle stress during hard seasons?

The letters Peter wrote to the dispersed in Asia Minor are full of short, encouraging pep-talks. For example, in this passage, he speaks of our living hope. The object and the effect of our hope are living. Hope enlivens and comforts; it helps us meet our difficulties face-on. These short but meaningful phrases are ripe for our meditation and for encouraging us in times of trouble.

Read 1 Peter 1:1-12.

Reading Questions

Who were the intended recipients of the letter and how were they described?

Peter says God has given us new birth in His mercy. What two gifts come with that new birth?

What inheritance is inferred in these verses?

What did Peter say was the purpose of trials and suffering?

Why were believers filled with inexpressible joy?

What did the prophets search intently for?

Old Testament Links

The tempering of believers through fire, or trials, by God is different from temptation by evil or sin. Satan's intentions are to see us fail, while God in his love desires to see us built up. Neither of the intentions, God's or Satan's, determine the outcome, as our personal responsibility is still part of the result of trials. Peter was encouraging the believers in Asia Minor to find joy and hope in suffering with the certainty of that hope and future inheritance with their new life.

According to 1 Samuel 10:6, what was responsible for new life? How did the Old Testament new life help clarify the context of verses 3 and 4?

Read Deuteronomy 8:2, 13:3 and Judges 2:22 to gain insight into God's motives for testing his people. Describe what that motive was in these cases.

Application

Note two verses from this passage which may encourage you in times of suffering or trials. Write them and put them in a place you will see them regularly and be reminded of God's presence in those times.

Draw a timeline of your life and note the times where trials occurred. Consider what joy has come because of or after those trials.

Session 2: An Old Identity Made New

1 Peter 1:13-2:10

Opening

What are two to three key tips to remaining impartial in judgment?

How would you define "sincere love"?

This portion of 1 Peter opens with writings on the application of Old Testament imagery to New Covenant believers. The idea of being holy, redeemed by the lamb, a new temple and a kingdom of priests all allude to the chosen people of God in the Old Testament. Yet Peter said each of these is also true for believers today. He lays down a challenge, exhorting us to live lives that are worthy of our belonging to God.

Read 1 Peter 1:13-2:10.

Reading Questions

What description of living holy is given in the text?

How were the readers of this letter redeemed?

How is purification described, and how is being born again described?

What must be done to "grow up in salvation" and what drove the believers to do so?

Describe the analogy of believers as "living stones".

What descriptors did Peter use in the final part of the passage to describe Christ followers?

Old Testament Links

Each reference that Peter used to place the believers of Asia Minor among God's chosen enriches our understanding of the life we have in Christ. The continuous thread of God's people from the beginning of history to the end runs through this passage as much as it runs through the whole Bible.

Read Deuteronomy 10:12-22 and note the parallel exhortations and identities between the passage for today's session.

Choose at least two of the following passages to review from the Old Testament passages that Peter referred to in his letter to the persecuted believers. What hope or encouragement do these passages impart to the letter's readers? Exodus 12:1-13, Exodus 19:3-8, Leviticus 20:7 and 26, Ezekiel 40:1-5.

Application

How do the images of the Old Testament chosen ones, the Israelites, apply to you today, how does it impact someone seeking to live holy?

Peter made it clear that new believers, not only the Israelites, belonged to God and were precious. How does this make you feel? How does this belonging help reframe past experiences of being left out?

Session 3: Living Godly Lives

1 Peter 2:11-3:7

Opening

Name three "dos" and three "don'ts" that would describe a godly life.

What does it mean to do something "for the Lord's sake?"

Peter urged his readers in this session's passage to focus on doing good toward others. He admitted that this was different from society and offered encouragement and examples to the readers to help them overcome doubts about being different. The lens

Peter used was that of Christ as he described the relationships that can be different.

Read 1 Peter 2:11-3:7.

Reading Questions

What encouragement is given to those who are accused of doing wrong in 1 Peter 2:11-12?

Who was instructed to submit to human authority?

Describe living "as God's slaves", according to the surrounding verses.

What example was given for slaves to follow? How was this presented in parallel to the life of slaves?

1 Peter 3:1 instructed wives to submit "in the same way". What way was it referring to?

Use your own words to describe how husbands were instructed to treat wives in 1 Peter 3:7.

Old Testament Links

This passage includes part of a "household code" which outlines the behavior expected of those in the household, including slaves. While some of the code was included in the Old Testament, others seem to address the culture of Asia Minor where the readers of 1 Peter lived. These instructions would assist in assuring local authorities that Christians would not subvert their culture, while also recognizing the situation of slaves as well as women and men who converted to Christianity.

How do Exodus 22:28 and Proverbs 24:21 agree with 1 Peter 2:13-17? How do they differ?

Read these three short passages and summarize the relationship shown - Genesis 16:1-4, 18:2, 9-12, 21:11-12.

Application

Today, slavery is banned in most countries. Do you think Peter agreed or disagreed with that stance? Explain your answer.

What household rules do you have in your house now, or would you like to have?

Session 4: Stewards of God's Grace

1 Peter 3:8-4:11

Opening

List some gifts that people use to serve the church, a business or their home life. Describe how some are God-given?

Suffering can be a difficult topic to discuss. What kind of suffering do people experience in life?

Peter continued the discourse on relationships and acknowledged the suffering that relationships sometimes bring. Tying us to Christ and his suffering, however, offered hope and potentially drew the readers nearer to Christ by identifying with him. Closing with another call to love one another underscores the importance of relationship in our lives, as in theirs.

Read 1 Peter 3:8-4:11.

Reading Questions

What is the blessing referenced in 1 Peter 3:9?

Describe the parallel of a believer's suffering and Christ's suffering.

Summarize what the passage says about baptism.

Who has submitted to Christ who is at God's right hand (1 Peter 3:21-22)?

What are some positives that come to those who "suffer in the body"?

How did Peter instruct followers to steward God's grace?

What are the exhortations that Peter gave to the believers about life in community (1 Peter 3:7-11)?

Old Testament Links

The Old Testament opened with God in relationship with Adam and Eve, but this relationship with humankind deteriorated. However, God didn't abandon his relationship with us; he instead has sought to bind us to him through his love. He has demonstrated his power and love in many ways and through words. Peter drew on some of those for his teachings as well.

Read Isaiah 8:11-14 and place it in the context of 1 Peter 3:14-15. How did the response to Isaiah's suffering under people's opinions or thoughts lead to hope? How did Peter also lead suffering toward hope in the surrounding verses?

Proverbs 10:12 and 17:9 also convey the idea that "love covers a multitude of sins". How do these three verses, including 1 Peter 4:8, help define love?

Application

What gentle and respectful answer do you have if someone asks you to "give the reason for the hope you have"?

What suffering have you undergone? How does Peter's identification of Jesus' suffering and yours make you feel?

Session 5: Share in Glory Revealed

1 Peter 4:12-5:14

Opening

On what occasions do you (1) rejoice, (2) feel blessed, or (3) praise God?

Define the word grace. Is there a difference between the secular and Christian use?

This reading brings the letter to a conclusion, summarizing the joy that believers can experience when suffering and giving notes to elders and churchgoers before closing. The reminder that suffering and grace go side-by-side may have encouraged believers of Asia Minor, and the crown of glory likely provided a future hope to remember in difficulties. We today can grasp the same from Peter today.

Read 1 Peter 4:12-5:14.

Reading Questions

The letter's readers were undergoing suffering for being Christians, yet Peter encouraged them to rejoice, know they are blessed and praise God. In what circumstances did he identify that they should be encouraged in these ways?

What should those who suffer do, according to 1 Peter 4:19?

How did Peter describe the attitude of an elder?

Summarize the comments about humility in 1 Peter 5:5-6.

What instructions are given regarding the devil?

In 1 Peter 5:12, it states, "this is the true grace of God." This seems to summarize the reason Peter wrote the letter. How would you summarize that idea?

Old Testament Links

The recipients of this letter were suffering and surely groaning as we see often in the Old Testament. Peter chose passages to remind the believers that they were accompanied by God who heard them in their difficulties.

The reference to humbling themselves offers the opportunity to consider their opposite, those who are proud. Read Proverbs 3:34, Isaiah 2:11-12, 17, Exodus 2:23-25 and 3:7-9, Judges 2:18, Judges 10:15-16. How are the humble and the suffering treated in these verses?

The devil is identified as one to resist in 1 Peter 5:8-9. Consider these passages about the enemy and list the characteristics described: Job 2:2, Proverbs 28:15, Ezekiel 22:25.

Application

All of the church members were called to "clothe themselves with humility," in 1 Peter 5:5. What makes it most difficult to do this? How can you take a step toward humbling yourself this week?

Given the above characteristics of the devil, consider how you can "resist him, standing firm in faith," (1 Peter 5:9).

Session 6: Character in Increasing Measure

2 Peter 1:1-21

Opening

How would you describe a Christian who is "effective" or "productive" in their knowledge of Christ?

List various ways that people use power. How is God's power similar or different from human power?

Peter opens this second letter to the church with a call for strengthening of character and certainty of salvation. As

Christians, we have been claimed by God as his own and we seek to further our Christlikeness; Peter laid out a bit of a roadmap to characteristics of Christlikeness and urged believers to hold fast to the promises that God has given regarding our salvation. These words stand true for us today.

Read 2 Peter 1:1-21.

Reading Questions

What was the grace and peace that Peter blessed readers with like? How did they receive this?

How has God provided believers with "everything we need for a godly life." (2 Peter 1:3)?

Peter listed several characteristics which believers possess. Why did he feel they were important? What did he say of those who did not possess these traits?

How did Peter describe Christ's coming and what He received when he came.

Why did Peter see prophetic message as important?

What did the Holy Spirt carry and what was the path starting and ending point?

Old Testament Links

Peters opening to this epistle reminded readers of God's consistency. From the Old Testament to the New Testament and even today, God is the same. He was called Savior and he spoke of salvation to come. As you consider the following questions, remember that God was Savior, is still Savior today, and will always be.

Read Psalm 85:4, Isaiah 45:15, 21, and Micah 7:7. What is God's title in these verses? How did Peter's use of the title confirm Jesus' divinity and saving nature?

Peter urged the readers to view the Scripture as completely reliable and then described it. Read Psalm 119:105, Isaiah 60:1, and Numbers 24:17. How were these passages unified, or rather who unites these verses?

Application

Peter says that God has given us all we need to live well for him (2 Peter 1:3). What is one area where you have been feeling under-resourced? How does this verse impact that feeling of lack?

In 2 Peter 1:10-11, Peter spoke of confirming your calling and election. What does that look like for you in practice? How do your choices reflect your commitment to Christ?

Session 7: Empty Words of False Teachers

2 Peter 2:1-22

Opening

Describe the result of incorrect information. How should someone deal with misinformation?

What are some reasons people might be drawn to persuasive but harmful leaders or ideas?

Turning from prophesy and reliability of the Scriptures, Peter wrote of false teachers. He spoke of how they would draw some believers into sin and of how they would bring their own destruction upon themselves. This chapter, however, also includes bright points of God's rescue of those who are surrounded by darkness and the ungodly. He remembers his people and rescues the godly. The promises the false teachers twist and corrupt, stand in God's light of love for us today as they did for those suffering in Peter's time.

Read 2 Peter 2:1-22.

Reading Questions

In Peter 2:1-3, list the examples of what false teachers were doing in that time.

Who did God not spare and who did he rescue from sin (2 Peter 2:4-10)? List at least three of each.

Describe how the bold and arrogant were compared to angels and animals.

What ungodly activities do these who are perishing carry out? List at least six activities from 2 Peter 2:13-19.

What was the condition of those who "have escaped corruption... and are again entangled" (2 Peter 2:20) compared to their previous state?

Old Testament Links

No fewer than five examples of depraved conduct from the Old Testament are used as illustrations in this passage. Thousands of years passed between those examples and the example of the depraved in Peter's time and thousands of years have passed since Peter wrote and we still have those today who behave similarly. Sin abounds now just as it did in the times of the Bible. Peter offered examples to warn the readers of the letter against being led astray from God and godliness, a warning we too can heed.

Read about the prophets in Jeremiah 6:14; 23:16-22,25-32; 28:9 and Ezekiel 13:3-10,16. Where did they get inspiration to speak and what did they speak of?

Genesis 6:1-13,18 told of the situation that surrounded Noah before the flood. How did it compare to the time of Peter? How did it compare to today?

Application

Peter's lists of how God rescues the godly and judges the unrighteous emphasize God's goodness. How does that truth make you feel in the face of injustice, evil, or deception?

Arrogance, greed, and sensuality are given as examples that lead people away from God. Which of the named temptations do you struggle with yourself? Which do you feel God has conquered in you?

Session 8: New Heaven, New Earth

2 Peter 3:1-18

Opening

What are some common situations when patience is needed or important?

How does waiting impact feelings about a plan? How does someone's understanding of time impact their decisions and feelings?

At last, Peter turned to the coming day of judgement for both the godly and the ungodly. The tone changes a bit from the previous gloom to shine a light of hope for the patience and loving judgement of God. He keeps his promises and the new creation is coming, Peter said. These are surely words of encouragement for us today.

Read 2 Peter 3:1-18.

Reading Questions

Why did Peter write these letters?

How did Peter connect God's power to impatience?

Describe how God views time according to Peter.

Peter used several metaphors to describe the day of the Lord, also called the day of judgement. What did he tell the readers to expect?

What kind of people did Peter think believers should be given that the end would come?

What promise did Peter use to remind believers of God's care for his people?

What warning regarding Paul's writings did Peter give?

Old Testament Links

Peter's emphasis on the prophets again showed as he spoke of the end days and the new creation. He affirmed his own belief in the reliability of the Scriptures by pointing to their words and the joy of God's judgement to come.

Read Isaiah 9:7, 11:4-5, 61:11, 65:17, 66:22 and identify the promises for God's people that Peter referenced in 2 Peter 3.

Read these prophets to understand the coming judgement for the ungodly: Isaiah 2:12, Joel 1:15, Amos 5:18-20. How might these references have encouraged the recipients of this epistle?

Application

Peter stated that some things in Paul's letters are hard to understand and may be distorted. What are some ways that you can grow in discernment of truth and false teaching?

Peter urged believers to be "at peace" with God (2 Peter 3:14). What aspects of your life are not peaceful right now? What can you do to bring peace to those areas?

Conclusion

Throughout these letters, Peter reminded people of God's judgement and promises yet to come. This was balanced by the attention on judgement of the ungodly.

Based on these teachings, how would you describe God's judgement?

Summarize the promises of the coming return of Christ?

What did you learn about God in this study?

What did you learn about yourself in this study?

Do you believe that Jesus is the Messiah, the Son of God and have you received life in his name? If so, describe the qualities of that life.

If this is the first time that you have answered yes to the call of following Jesus, please reach out to a local church or the author to share of your choice and find support for your new life.

To continue your deep dive into "Seeing the Old Testament in the Epistles", pick up Revelation to continue your study. Find it at your nearest retailer by scanning the QR code today.

Revelation:
Worship
the
Lamb

Also By Sarah K. Howley

Seeing the Old Testament in the Epistles
Ephesians: Experience God's Power
James: Know God's Wisdom
1&2 Thessalonians: Prepare for Christ's Return
Hebrews: Elevate Jesus

The Son Reveals the Father
I Am: An 8-Session Study of John
Heart: A 12-Session Study of Luke
Word: An 11-Session Study of Matthew
King: An 8-Session Study of Mark
Our Trustworthy God: How Much God loves You, Joyfully
Engages with You, and Trusts You

Women of the Old Testament Bible Studies
Hope: A Bible Study of Women in Jesus' Lineage
Faith (coming 2025)
Love (coming 2026)

Alive Again Bible Study on Forgiveness
Alive Again: Find Healing in in Forgiveness
Alive Again Bible Study: Find Healing in Forgiveness
Alive Again Forgiveness Prayer Journal

About the Author

Sarah K. Howley is a Bible teacher, passionate about helping believers grow spiritually and take on the character of Christ. She is the founder of InspiritEncourage, an author, speaker, and trained Christian counselor. She has lived in over five countries on four continents and takes her own espresso wherever she goes. Sarah and her husband support initiatives for feeding the hungry and for expanding access to reading.

You can find Sarah on Facebook and Instagram @inspiritencourage. To book Sarah as a speaker at your next event, please contact her through her website. For weekly encouragement and information on her latest releases, sign up for Sarah's newsletter at InspiritEncourage.com.

InspiritEncourage

www.ingramcontent.com/pod-product-compliance
Lightning Source LLC
Chambersburg PA
CBHW051002140626
46546CB00017B/2693